# Motivation to Last a Lifetime

# Motivation to Last a Lifetime

Ted W. Engstrom

President
World Vision

with
Robert C. Larson

Zondervan Publishing House
Grand Rapids, Michigan

Daybreak Books are published by Zondervan
Publishing House, 1415 Lake Drive, S.E.,
Grand Rapids, Michigan 49506

MOTIVATION TO LAST A LIFETIME
Copyright © 1984 by The Zondervan Corporation
1415 Lake Drive, S.E.Grand Rapids, Michigan 49506

**Library of Congress Cataloging in Publication Data**

Engstrom, Theodore Wilhelm, 1916–
    Motivation to last a lifetime.

    Includes bibliographical references.
    1.   Christian life—1960–        .  2.   Motivation (Psy-
chology)   I.   Larson, Robert C.   II.   Title.
BV4501.2.E583   1984            248.4            83-23371

ISBN 0-310-24251-7 (paper)
ISBN 0-310-24250-9 (cloth)

Edited by Julie Ackerman Link

*Printed in the United States of America*

87   88   89   90 / 10   9   8   7   6   5   4   3

# Contents

# Foreword

*Motivation to Last a Lifetime* has the potential to be a special gift from God to all who read it. Without a doubt, lack of motivation is one of the great challenges of our society. Few of us seem to live up to our potential.

In fact, many of us would be delighted simply to muster enough motivation for the tasks that await us this day. To believe we can receive enough motivation to last a lifetime seems too good to be true. This little volume, however, offers lasting motivation to all who will heed the wise and godly counsel of its author.

I have known Ted Engstrom for nearly twenty-five years. I have seen him in the role of father, husband, board member, public speaker, administrator, teacher, leader, and, most closely, personal friend. Without a doubt, he is one of the most motivated and effective servants of Jesus Christ I have ever known. Ted models what he writes. This volume does not contain mere theory—it teaches practical stuff that will work in our lives if we put it into action.

Above all, Ted Engstrom guides us to the ultimate source of motivation—Jesus Christ. To receive Christ as Savior and to follow Him as Lord is the key to spiritual and practical motivation. The Lordship of Christ in our lives provides the gift of the Holy Spirit, the ultimate motivator. He will help us take the clear and positive steps Dr. Engstrom outlines for us. Indeed, through this book, we can find enough motivation to last us a lifetime.

PAUL A. CEDAR
PASTOR, LAKE AVENUE CONGREGATIONAL CHURCH
PASADENA, CALIFORNIA

*Life, if anything, is an endless process of self-discovery.*

# 1

# The Discovery

**D**r. Victor E. Frankl, survivor of three grim years at Auschwitz and other Nazi prisons, has recorded his observations on life in Hitler's camps:

> We who lived in concentration camps can remember the men who walked through the huts comforting others, giving away their last piece of bread. They may have been few in number, but they offer sufficient proof that everything can be taken from a man but one thing: the last of the human freedoms—to choose one's attitude in any given set of circumstances, to choose one's own way.

And there are always choices to make. Every day, every hour, offered the opportunity to make a decision, a decision which determined whether you would or would not submit to those powers which threatened to rob you of your very self, your inner freedom; which determined whether or not you would become the plaything of circumstance, re-nouncing freedom and dignity to become molded into the form of the typical inmate.

. . . Even though conditions such as lack of sleep, insufficient food and various mental stresses may suggest that the inmates were bound to react in certain ways, in the final analysis it becomes clear that the sort of person the prisoner became was the result of an inner decision, and not the result of camp influences alone. Fundamentally, therefore, any man can, even under such circumstances, de-cide what shall become of him—mentally and spir-itually.[1]

Some of you who hold this small book in your hands know firsthand the suffering of those con-centration camps. Most of us escaped the terror of that blight on human history. But whether we've been forced to endure the horror and indescribable pain of personal torture or not, all of us can grap-ple with Dr. Frankl's statement that fundamen-tally, under life's most trying pressures, it is the obligation of every man and woman to decide what to do with his or her life—mentally and physically. No exceptions. Period! Such a decision then gives way to what life is really all about—discovery.

What a tremendous, invigorating word— *Discovery!* More colorful than "find" or "locate" or "come up with." The word "discovery" has in-trigue. Mystery. It implies that something valuable—even precious—is temporarily hidden from normal view, just waiting for us to dig until we find it.

As you begin this book, I want to help you start to make the kinds of personal discoveries that will affect how you live the rest of your life. You may be a high school, college, or seminary student, a realtor, clergyman, housewife, computer expert, electrician, executive—it doesn't really matter. Because what is written in these pages is meant for you.

Consider this. If you were to participate in an archeological expedition, you would need certain essentials, including the strong mental desire to *believe* something is there to discover, and the assurance that the treasure, no matter how hidden, will yield to your desire to bring it to the surface.

Then you would need specific tools—made just for digging in the way *you* choose to dig. Without the right tools you may not make any discovery at all.

The task of digging would have to take absolute priority over every other activity in your life. You cannot scrape a few inches of dirt for five minutes a day and expect to make much of a discovery. You might uncover a few commonplace arrowheads— but you would, in all probability, *miss the gold.* And every day, good, sincere, well-meaning people everywhere are missing the gold.

Our search in these pages is not for gold or oil or ancient Spanish pieces of eight, although what we find could well be worth a hundred—even a thousand—times more than such wealth. Rather, we are about to discover ways to determine—and put into action—what can motivate us to become the very best God intends us to be. And when we make that important discovery, only the sky above will be our limit.

Let us initially talk about self-motivation, and let me suggest fourteen ways to begin the process.

1. *Determine values.* Motivation is always closely related to our own value systems, desires, needs, and ambitions. So we ask ourselves, What do I value most? What consumes my time? What are my deepest needs? How am I doing in fulfilling them?

We've read stories of men and women who have left high-level, lucrative, executive positions to run grocery stores or fishing tackle shops in the mountains. Whether it was a mid-life crisis or just a determination to get out of the rat race, their decisions to make a change started with the questions, What do I value most? and How can I go about getting that for me?

2. *Realize motivation is continuous.* We are always motivated in some direction—good or bad—to do something. So right now, as we begin, let's ask ourselves, What is my direction? Where am I heading? If money or location or health or anything else were not obstacles, what would I do with my life—beginning today?

Another way to ask ourselves that question might be, What would I like to have written on my tombstone? Since that would be my final statement, it obviously would be an important one concerning the direction I had wanted my life to take.

3. *Seek wisdom.* We must recognize and understand that divine wisdom is the only thing that has true value. In James 1:5, the apostle James admonishes us that "if any of you lacks wisdom, he should ask God, who gives generously to all without finding fault, and it will be given him." Wise counsel indeed! Read the words of Solomon the Wise. God enabled him to share practical wisdom with each of us—even these millennia after God revealed His wisdom to His servant Solomon.

4. *Be realistic about limitations.* We must be sure to set goals within our reach. Attempting the impossible will destroy our motivation overnight. Rome wasn't built in a day. Neither is a career . . . nor a life that's worth living.

Yes, we must stretch ourselves, but we must also ask, Is this goal I'm contemplating in sync with who I am? Will I be compatible in this new environment? Does my intuition tell me I may be overextending myself and my abilities in this?

We are neither superman nor wonderwoman. And if we feel we must do everything, sooner or later we will make the startling discovery that we are doing absolutely nothing of lasting value.

5. *Be willing to take some risks.* We cannot be afraid to try new ideas and new methods and we need to challenge with a vengeance such killer phrases as, "You're on the wrong track"; "The boss ought to get a chuckle out of *that* idea"; "Hey, I can tell you, the twelfth floor isn't going to like it";

"Someday there may be a need for this"; and the biggest putdown of all, "What are you, some kind of nut?" Charles H. Clark, in his fine pamphlet "Idea Management: How to Motivate Creativity and Innovation," offers helpful suggestions in the whole arena of self-motivation.

Don't forget! All the new ways of doing things have not yet been discovered. So take some risks, find a better way. Maybe you will invent a new mousetrap in the process!

6. *Make lists.* If each of us had to make a decision today that would change the direction of our lives, what would it be? Would we start our own business? Take an overseas assignment? Work in a halfway house for kids in trouble? Would we finally sit down and write that novel? Start a course in accounting at night school? Take flying lessons? Start big. Think blue sky. No limits.

Make a list of your grandest dreams and then put it aside—but don't forget it. Make another list with the heading "Things I can start doing today." Be specific, clear, and realistic. A good and effective, easily described plan (written so both you and others can understand it) is very highly motivational.

7. *Pray.* We must lay our plans before the Lord. Years ago I took Psalm 32:8 as my life verse. "I will instruct thee and teach thee in the way that thou shalt go; I will guide thee with mine eye" (KJV). The knowledge that God does instruct, teach, and lead His children step by step and day by day is a constant encouragement to me. He is far more in-

terested in us, our plans, our future, and our well-being than we are ourselves, and we must pray about what we think God has for us in this process. He is as much concerned about the minutia in our planning as He is about the final results. More is accomplished by prayer than by anything else this world knows. Prayer must be an integral part of our desire for redemptive motivation in our life.

Who can explain prayer? We have direct access to the Maker of the universe. We can call on Him, counsel with Him. God, in His Word, continually invites us into His presence. "Call on me . . ." "We have an advocate with the Father, even Jesus Christ the righteous one." God's way of working always is in answer to believing prayer!

8. *Divide project into manageable parts.* After we've given thought and prayer to our direction, we must ask ourselves, How can I break this up into manageable pieces so I can handle it effectively? Remaining consistently self-motivated throughout life comes from rewarding ourselves with successes every day. But if we overload our circuits, our system will begin to close down— physically and emotionally. When that happens we will frustrate ourselves into a corresponding loss of productivity. So initially, we must take only bite-size chunks and not try to finish a six-month project in six weeks. Being realistic with ourselves about our abilities will pay off in the long run.

9. *Take action.* Procrastination is the death blow to self-motivation. "I'll do it later . . . after I

get organized" is the language of the unsuccessful and the frustrated. Successful, highly motivated men and women don't put it off. They know their lives are no more than the accumulation of precious seconds, minutes, and days—golden moments never to be recaptured.

Just three words, *Do it now,* can propel us on to achievements we never thought possible. *Do it now!* is a worthy motto for all of life. Start prospecting a new client, *now.* Empty the garbage, *now.* Fix the leak in the sink, or in the roof, *now.* Love your spouse, *now.* Today unused is lost forever, and tomorrow may never come.

10. *Consider the negative consequences of inaction.* After establishing practical goals and objectives for our lives, we need to remind ourselves of the horrors of letting ourselves down—financial loss, depression, loss of momentum in business, deteriorating health, taking out frustrations on loved ones.

When we choose to *do it now,* we cut through our work like a machete going through high brush. When we choose not to act, our inaction takes on a life of its own and inflicts its punishment on us.

11. *Take advantage of energy peaks.* All of us need to learn to schedule our most important tasks during those times when our body and mind are functioning at top level. Some of us are morning persons, others don't get going until midnight. Some need naps, others don't. Only you know when you work at your best and highest level. It

may be helpful to make an "energy chart" for the month.

At the end of each day, make a note of those periods of time when you did your most productive work. Was it after a nap? After lunch? Ufter a stimulating conversation with an associate or with one of your children?

This regular, personal survey of our top moments will help give us the insights to keep us self-motivated for a lifetime.

12. *Trust in a big God.* God is without limits. Nothing is impossible with Him. He is the author of true creativity. All creation is His, including every idea our minds can conceive. He keenly desires to give us the ability to make the right choices in our lives.

13. *Become accountable.* Find some other person—or a small group of people—whom you trust and who trust you. There is a great deal of pleasure in being held accountable, yet many of us fear this exposure. It is good to share our victories with others. But at the same time, most of us know that the joy of anticipated success can turn to ashes in the day of failure. Yet, success is only possible if the potential for failure exists.

There are three kinds of accountability. The first is determined by the society into which we are born. To be a part of our society, we must accept the accountability society places on us. We are, of course, expected to do certain things correctly and according to schedule. Taxes will come due every April. Stoplights will turn red. The consequences of ignoring these occurrences are powerful incentives for us to perform well. Accountability is assumed. It is a given, not an option.

We accept the second kind of accountability when we join an organization, whether it is part of our vocation or something like our local church. When we accept a job, we automatically accept responsibility to our superiors, peers, and subordinates. We may play different roles at different times, one time as leader, another time as follower, but accountability is always part of the job. Too often in our service we forget that.

The third kind of accountability is that which we voluntarily make to others. In many ways it is the most effective. We all seem to perform better against the goals we set for ourselves. This kind of accountability can operate in a number of ways. At the organizational level, it works for the superior who not only invites his subordinates to share in setting their own goals but who invites his subordinates to hold *him* accountable for *his* goals.

At the one-to-one, person-to-person level, we should seek to be accountable to someone for as many areas of our life as possible and to permit others to ask us to hold them accountable. I have a friend who often asks the simple question, "What can I pray about for you this week?" I soon learned that he intended to accept responsibility not only to pray about that need, but later to ask, "How did it go?" I quickly learned not to be too glib with my prayer requests!

14. *Be optimistic.* Success is won by people who

know it can be done. One of the greatest salesmen of all time, W. Clement Stone, has said repeatedly, "What the mind can conceive and believe in, the mind can achieve." *And Stone is right!*

Do we believe it? Do we dare believe it? If we do, it will change our lives. We will be able to aim higher and reach further than we ever thought possible, because the self-motivated optimist is getting things done when others are still wondering if they *can* be done.

Optimists are self-motivated by inspiring themselves to action. They believe in who they are and in what they are doing. They make mistakes and learn from them. They achieve success but don't take for granted that success will come again. They set long-range objectives, but they also encourage themselves with daily personal rewards.

Optimists know that with God's help they *can* be the people they were created to be. We can be open, free, caring, spontaneous—with the daily awareness that successful living is nothing if not, with God's help, an endless journey in self-discovery and personal fulfillment.

God made man to go by motives,
and he will not go without them,
any more than a boat without
steam or a balloon without gas.
                    Henry Ward Beecher

# 2

# Finding Motives to
# Keep You Going
## (False Motivation Won't Last)

**S**everal years ago *Newsweek* ran an immensely valuable two-page piece entitled "Advice to a (Bored) Young Man" in its "Responsibility Series." Despite its title, its counsel is to us all—man or woman, young or old.

> Died, age 20; buried, age 60. The sad epitaph of too many Americans. Mummification sets in on too many young men at an age when they should be ripping the world wide open. For example: Many people reading this page are doing so with the aid of bifocals. Inventor? *B. Franklin*, age 79.
>
> The presses that printed this page were powered by electricity. One of the first harnessers? *B. Franklin*, age 40.

Some are reading this on the campus of one of the Ivy League universities. Founder? *B. Franklin,* age 45.

Others, in a library. Who founded the first library in America? *B. Franklin,* age 25.

Some got their copy through the U.S. Mail. Its father? *B. Franklin,* age 31.

Now, think fire. Who started the first fire department, invented the lightning rod, designed a heating stove still in use today? *B. Franklin,* ages 31, 43, 36.

Wit. Conversationalist. Economist. Philosopher. Diplomat. Printer. Publisher. Linguist (spoke and wrote five languages). Advocate of paratroopers (from balloons) a century before the airplane was invented. All this until age 84.

And he had exactly two years of formal schooling. It's a good bet that you already have more sheer knowledge than Franklin ever had when he was your age.

Perhaps you think there's no use trying to think of anything new, that everything's been done. Wrong. The simple, agrarian America of Franklin's day didn't begin to need the answers we need today.

Go do something about it.[1]

*Newsweek* then suggested that the reader tear out the page and "read it on *your* 84th birthday. Ask yourself what took over in your life: indolence or ingenuity?"

I'm not suggesting you tear out this page, but we all need to keep it handy. There's no reason, however, to wait until our eighty-fourth birthdays. How about looking at it every birthday—or every month—or every week for the rest of our lives!

Benjamin Franklin found motives to keep him going for a lifetime of service to his country and to his fellow-man. And with each success his motivation became even stronger.

Are you saying, "Come on, now, you can't expect me to be a Benjamin Franklin." Or are you thinking, "Now there was a great man. And I have just as much opportunity to make my life count as he did." We hope it's the latter. Because, for one thing, it's true.

We *do* have as much opportunity. And those diamonds still *can* be found in our own backyard. We just need to know where to dig.

So we need to ask ourselves, What are my motives? What makes me want to dig and discover and explore and learn? What are my objectives, my goals? What contributions am I making—or do I plan to make—to my family, my society, myself?

Much of what motivates us is little more than *herd mentality.* It's on the best-seller list, so we read it. It's on the cover of our favorite magazine, so we wear it. It's featured in the gardening magazine, so we grow it. A superstar touts it on television, so we buy it, or rent it, or eat it, or fly it!

All this is wonderful. But life is more than knee-jerk responses to someone's marketing ideas. And we will never know the thrill of a life well lived until we engage ourselves in the lifelong pursuit of motives that keep us going.

If Thoreau was right in saying "all men lead lives of quiet desperation," and if that is the story of *our* lives, then we may as well take early orders for our epitaphs, which might read:

> Here lies John . . . here lies Mary
> From very young to very old
> They always did what they were told.

In all their years of living on this earth they never chose to learn how to live. Instead of soaring to the heavens, pressing, pushing, extending themselves just a little further, they chose to stay earthbound.

All of us knew athletes in high school or college who had tremendous natural ability—who could have been true "stars" in their sports—but who just didn't have the drive or urge or willingness to push themselves, and thus remained "second-stringers." We also know of people with truly brilliant minds who could be successful scientists or researchers or leaders in one of many disciplines, but who simply won't pay the price for such readily achievable success. Tragic!

Let's look at some guidelines that are essential for a lifetime of personal fulfillment.

*Keep our reservoirs full.* We must store up compassion, encouragement, forgiveness, and hope so we will have enough to give to others when they need it.

What an example Mother Teresa in Calcutta is for each of us. Born of poor Albanian parents in Yugoslavia, she determined early in life to give herself completely to God in order to minister to "the poorest of the poor" in the wretched slums of that Indian city. And for decades she has unreservedly shared of herself so that thousands rise up and call her blessed. A Nobel Prize winner, she remains the simple, modest peasant woman, who, through her deep and unswerving devotion and commitment, has been motivated to this exemplary service for our Lord Jesus Christ.

Mother Teresa said that each of us has a mission to fulfill, a mission of love, but that it must begin in our homes . . . in the place where we are, with the people with whom we are the closest, and then spread out. What wise advice this is indeed.

*Work on our character.* Many men and women are so concerned with their reputations that they give little or no thought to the development of their most important possession: their character. Do we know who we really are? Are we well-defined persons? Have we established standards for our lives on which we simply refuse to compromise? (Remember, reputation only functions under favorable circumstances; character functions under unfavorable circumstances.)

If answering such questions is difficult, try this exercise. Pretend you are a reporter on special assignment to do a cover story on *you.* That's right, *you.*

For a full working day, *you* the reporter will cover *you* the person. What will you discover as you follow yourself to the office, the gym, the kitchen, the television set? Report accurately all you see.

Although much of what you observe may make you want to put your pencil and pad down, you are required to complete the assignment.

Observe yourself in the supermarket lane marked "10 items only" when the person in front of you has eleven items (you know because you counted them).

At the office, report on how you treat your employees, how you talk on the telephone, how "sincerely" you sign your letters, and how your pulse rate rises when the IRS says you are being audited.

Would you be willing to make your story a cover story? What kind of man or woman emerges? Do you like what apparently motivates you?

In my forty-year ministry, I have traveled annually to every nook and cranny and corner of the world, and I have met "unsung" heroes whose exemplary character, dedication, and determination to be at their best for God (even though seemingly no one would be aware of it) have challenged me time without number. But God sees and knows. And in eternity that's what will really matter!

*Seek good health.* Maybe it's time you reactivated that membership in your local *Y*, or started playing tennis or golf again. How long has it been since you've had a physical? Do you like the profile you see in the mirror each morning? Or ought you to lose a few pounds?

Here on earth, your body is a most prized possession. If it is not functioning properly, it's going to be difficult to be motivated about anything.

We know our bodies inevitably become what our minds harbor. In fact, the correlation between the "state of the mind" and the "physical condition of the body" is so strong it's now estimated that seventy percent of all Americans go to doctors for treatment when they have nothing physically wrong.

Reports indicate that fifty-two percent of American men and women are seeing psychologists or psychiatrists or are going to great expense at a vast assortment of mental health clinics—when it's essentially their thinking that's all wrong.

Spiritual balance is often neglected as a factor that affects our emotional life and brings about stability. Recognize how vital it is to spend time with God, in His Word, and in fellowship with fellow believers. We dare not stand alone. God has committed Himself to us. Draw daily upon His reserves.

*Be enthusiastic about life.* "But I can't get worked up about things; it's just not my nature," some say. "I work hard all day, like to come home and watch a little TV, and then go to bed. It's just not like me to get all excited about anything."

Well, we had all better find *something* to excite us . . . and we'd better find it fast. At least we can be grateful we got up this morning. Lots of people didn't! When we breathed on the bathroom mirror today, it fogged up. That's terrific. That's something to get worked up about.

But we can't stop there. Now that we've confirmed we are alive, we must do something with this wonderful day, these precious minutes. We must find something to live for—perhaps even something to die for. It will change our lives.

*Be a person of faith.* Do we have the kind of faith that can move mountains? Perhaps they won't be the Sierras or the Himalayas. But what about the mountains of pain, worry, fear, and hopelessness all around us?

William Carey, often called the father of modern missions, was such a person of faith. Carey left his cobbler's bench in Britain almost two centuries ago to serve as a pioneer missionary in India. He knew no one there; he had no idea what he would face; he had no knowledge of the languages. When he died, after more than forty years of ministry in India, he had translated the Bible into three major Indian languages, had founded what has become the largest newspaper in India, had established the strong and effective Baptist Church Union in India, had founded what has become the largest seminary in India, and had done more than any individual to bring the message of the Gospel of Christ to that sub-continent. He was one simple cobbler who took God at His word, and his obedience immeasurably affected an entire subcontinent.

*Be a friend.* We all know barbers and beauticians are often the best "poor person's psychologist." They listen while they cut and comb. Over the years they often become real friends with their clients.

We can be the same kind of person to *our* friends by helping them focus on what is bothering them. We can help put their problem in perspective, perhaps even suggest another way of looking at the disturbing issue. But we must take time to listen and make ourselves available. All the empathy, all the skill in the world are of no value if the person who needs our ear cannot get it. Times to listen can obviously be scheduled, but most of the important times come quite unexpectedly. Accept them when they come—and learn from listening.

Many people are still reluctant to seek counseling, and this is where we can help. We can listen with sympathetic gestures and mannerisms. By listening and caring we may help a friend overcome many unsettling fears. Have you noticed that those who often motivate us to action are usually those closest to us—our friends? And similarly, as we build friendships, we become "enablers" in the arena of motivation as we encourage our friends to participate in profitable and redemptive activities.

For serious problems, professional help is obviously necessary. But we don't need a wall filled with diplomas to be the best friend a person ever had.

*Learn to be calm under pressure.* A liberal endowment of patience is essential when pressures mount, as they inevitably will. The impatient person will become weakened and defective. "Be strong—and of a good courage" is God's word to Joshua—and to us.

The story is told of a young boy who wanted desperately to become a singer, but his teacher gave him no hope, telling him, "Son, you sound like the wind in the shutters!" But the boy's mother believed in her son—so much so that she sent him to another teacher. To pay the cost of her son's lessons she often went without shoes—sometimes even without food. The boy was Enrico Caruso. He became the greatest tenor of his time—because his mother loved him, had faith in him, and exercised patience.

*Be curious about life.* Develop an exploratory mind. Read. Ask questions. Listen. The exploring mind and heart adds spice to life. Those who turn over stones find the serendipities that make life fascinating. Let your curiosity "get the better of you" sometimes. It becomes the salt and pepper of life. Curiosity may have killed the cat, but it also enhances our lives.

*Invest in ourselves.* This is the only way we will be able to invest in others. Each of us is that important. There are *no* unimportant people in God's economy. Somewhere along the line a strange idea has developed that in order to be humble we also have to be mediocre. Where we get such an idea is a mystery. It certainly does not come from Scripture. Over and over again God selected ordinary people and made them extraordinary. Whether it was Moses of the Old Testament, with his heritage and palace training, or Paul in the New Testament, with his knowledge and organizational ability, God made them the best. And He will do the same for us. Know that this is so and accept the very best that God has for you. *You are* important!

The list could go on. But this is a start in the right direction in establishing goals and motives to last a lifetime. Much of what we've said thus far refers to self-growth—keeping our *own* reservoir full. But the highest motives of all are those that cause us to reach out to others.

Still, the best-laid plans—the strongest, most God-honoring desires—do go astray. That's when it's time to ask the next question: What do I do when I've lost my motivation?

Life is now in session. Are you
present?

B. Copeland

# 3

# What to Do When You've
# Lost Your Motivation

The sales manager of the Fido Dog Food Company grasped the podium firmly as he prepared
to speak to his salespeople at their weekly motivational meeting. In voice loud and clear, he
shouted, "Ladies and gentlemen of Fido Dog Food
Company, who's got the best packaging in the
country?"

As expected, everyone cheered, "We do!"

The sales manager continued, "Who's got the
best, most dynamic, most aggressive sales force?"

"We do!" came the enthusiastic reply.

Finally the boss asked, "Then why is it we're
number seventeen out of a total of eighteen dog
food companies in this country?"

Silence. People cleared their throats, searched for windows to look out of, played with their pencils.

Finally, a squeaky voice at the back of the room broke the silence with the memorable words, "Sir, it's because dogs don't like us!"

And not only dogs shift with the times, change their desires, get burned out or turned off; it happens to us all.

Once we knew where we were going. We pursued our goals with a vengeance. Now we're not so sure. Self-doubts have eroded our confidence. We've begun to slip and we really don't know why. Once satisfied, enthusiastic, and highly motivated, we're now depressed, ill-at-ease, plagued with the vague sense of having "missed the boat."

What action can we take to put things right? Let's look at some possibilities:

*Read inspirational books; listen to motivational cassettes.* These will help inspire us to action. No matter how bright, gifted, or intelligent we are, we can always use the insights of someone else. If we observe any person who has achieved success, we discover a person who has *worked at staying motivated.* Motivation is not automatic.

If we lose our drive and feel we are all washed up, with no more worlds to conquer, perhaps we've just lost our perspective. Because there still *are* worlds to conquer—hundreds of them—and there's one just waiting for each of us to discover.

We may have to take a thousand steps before we find it; but unless we take those thousand steps, we may never find that world waiting for us. So let's get a map and start moving. It's no sin to spend *some* time down in the dumps, but there is nothing saintly about *staying* there.

The Bible continually illustrates for us those men of faith who, at some point, seem to have lost their motivation. Look at Jonah on his way to Nineveh. Or Moses during his "backside of the desert" experience. Or Peter as he denied his Lord. These men were about to give up, but as God moved upon them they became, once again, very highly motivated. It can be so with us during our inevitable low periods. Our God is our Motivator!

*Recognize that we are always in the process of change.* A Greek philosopher said, "It is not possible to step twice into the same river." The water moves downstream, never to return. The man or woman brings new experiences to every new situation. Things may look the same, but they *never* are.

We may think we are working in the same office we worked in five years ago, but we're not. We may think we have the same boss, but we don't. Everything is in flux. And whether we realize it or not, this constant change has its effect on us all.

Those who think we are not living through times of traumatic change should spend an evening reading *Future Shock* or *The Third Wave* by Alvin Toffler or *New Rules* by Daniel Yankelovich.

Management expert Peter Drucker writes compellingly of the changes in what he calls our "Turbulent Times." Seminars on how to cope with change are promoted at every turn. Change, obviously, is threatening but inevitable. A highly motivated person understands this and continually adjusts to it.

The literature that describes our rapidly changing present and inevitable future continues to pound away at one thought—things will never be the way they once were, no matter how much we may long for the "good old days."

Perhaps our sense of "lost motivation" is no more than a resistance to the changes that come into our lives uninvited. Of the total numbers of Americans out of work, fifty percent of them will not find the jobs they are seeking, for those jobs will never again exist. Retraining, for them, is essential for economic survival.

That may be where *you* are. The old shoe no longer fits. The new wine splits the cask that held the old wine without spilling a drop. We all change—and will continue to change. We may not welcome it, like it, or even enjoy it. But we must accept it! If not, we're destined to live out our frustrations like good old Charlie Brown, who complained, "How can I do new math with an old math brain?" It doesn't take much reflection to know the answer: Learn new math!

*Don't try too hard.* Even though change is a necessary and inevitable part of life, we often try to cope with it in the wrong way. For instance, some of us may try too hard to become a success, becoming instead, burned out. A pastor tries to infuse life into a struggling, non-responsive congregation. A mother with the words "Super Mom" on her license plate frame tries hard to do everything—cook, bake, clean, be chauffeur for soccer and Little League and, on top of all that, tries to be the perfect wife. Pastor, wife, student, secretary—it doesn't matter—we may simply be trying too hard.

If you feel you are, the "slight edge" principle may help.

If you're an executive, work for a twelve percent increase in your company's production by raising it one percent each month. A twelve-percent increase may be frightening, even intimidating. But one percent a month is manageable—and possible.

Spend just fifteen minutes a day on a subject that will enhance your present position. Become an expert. Read every book on the subject you can lay your hands on. Spend time in the stacks at the library. Quietly become the most well-informed person in your field. You can do it—and it will only take fifteen minutes a day. But you must do it every day. It's a sure way to recapture a motivation to serve you for a lifetime.

Spend an equal time in the Scriptures each day. Ask God to give you the insight, energy, compassion, and wisdom you need. Check frequently the wisdom of Solomon in Proverbs; identify with the sweet singer of Israel, David, in the Psalms. It's still true: "Seek and you will find; knock and the door will be opened to you" (Matt. 7:7). Maybe it's time for you to start believing what you say you believe.

In his book *The Range of Human Capacities*, well-known psychologist Dr. David Wechsler says, "The differences that separate the masses of mankind from one another—with respect to any one or all of their capabilities—are small. As compared with other ratios or orders or differences met in nature, they are pitifully insignificant."[1]

Wechsler's message is clear. The successful person is usually only a little bit better than the one who fails. Why? Because he or she has chosen to take the "slight edge." Small differences—big results. This is one of the best antidotes we know for frustration and lack of motivation.

*Don't wish for life to get easier; pray to become stronger.*

Isaiah 40:31 should be a daily reminder of what happens when we go to the source of all true strength: "But they that wait upon the Lord shall renew their strength; they shall mount up with wings as eagles; they shall run, and not be weary; and they shall walk, and not faint" (KJV).

That is the secret of living. But to the believer it shouldn't be a secret at all. It's the heart of the Christian faith. A return to *real living.* No longer do we need to prop ourselves up with things we *hope* will carry us through. No. Pray for God's strength, and then believe it will come to you. We've gone through thousands of years of history since Isaiah made his declaration, but it remains as fresh as today's headlines: My strength comes from the Lord who made heaven and earth.

He also made you. And He made you to succeed.

Judged by the world's standards, not every incident of life can be termed a success, of course. But God's will for us is, as we daily walk with Him, that we will have success as He marks it—in the satisfaction of knowing that we are "the apple of His eye."

*Take a vacation.* Football coach Vince Lombardi once said, "Fatigue makes cowards of us all." That's true, isn't it? How many times have you just been too tired to plug ahead? Too wiped out to continue even another five minutes?

Perhaps you need to spend a few days walking a quiet beach, exploring the beauty of God's handiwork. Grab a handful of sand and let the grains run through your fingers. Remember God already has those grains counted. Then reflect a bit more. That same God knows and loves *you!*

Or head off for the mountains, the wilderness. Enjoy the beauty of silence. Let the Father speak to you in the stillness—away from the telephones, copy machines, telexes, soccer games, or preparations for the morning sermon. Carve out a few extra hours for a good book or for some special— and extra—time with the Lord.

Don't wait until next year to take such a vacation. Do it now, even if it is for only a few hours, days, or a weekend at a time. It will do more good than worry, aspirin, or black coffee.

*Re-evaluate goals.* Write down who you were ten years ago, five years ago, last year at this time. How have you changed? Are you reading the same kinds of books? Do you have new friends? Do you

still want the same things, value the same relationships?

You may discover you have changed more than
you thought possible.

It is terribly important that we continually re-
view our goals, our objectives, because they, as
well as we, do indeed change. Dr. Ari Kiev, Clinical
Professor of Psychiatry at Cornell University, in his
fine little book *Strategy for Daily Living,* says,

> The establishment of a goal is the key to suc-
> cessful living. In my practice as a psychiatrist, I
> have found that helping people to develop personal
> goals has proved to be the most effective way to help
> them cope with problems. Observing the lives of
> people who have mastered adversity, I have noted
> that they have established goals and sought with all
> their efforts to achieve them. From the moment
> they decided to concentrate all their energies on a
> specific objective, they began to summit the most
> difficult odds.

*Practice, practice, practice.* Fritz Kreisler, the
famed concert violinist, maintained a rigorous,
no-nonsense, eight-hour-daily practice schedule
throughout his long, outstanding musical career.
Often he would be asked why he needed to carry on
such vigorous practice sessions. After all, wasn't
he the best—without peer?

Kreisler had but one reply to such a question: "If
I neglect to practice for a month, my audience
knows the difference. If I neglect it for a week, my
wife knows the difference. If I neglect practice for a
day, Fritz Kreisler knows the difference."

When we think we've made it, we probably haven't. For often, when we've been blessed with even moderate success, we're tempted to lay down the tools that brought us to where we are. Tools such as perseverance, humility, caring for others, the ability to listen and empathize—and just plain hard work.

Paul Meyer, an authority on self-improvement through personal motivation, gives five danger signals that indicate our motivation is not what it once was.

*Doubt*—questioning our ability to do the job. Self-confidence is lost; worry and confusion take over.

*Procrastination*—putting off important decisions; hesitating to take considered risks; hoping the problem will take care of itself.

*Devotion to false symbols*—surrendering to egotism and status seeking; coveting the title of the job instead of concentrating on better ways and new ideas for actually doing the job; desiring to be a "well-thought-of" person instead of a thinking one.

*Complacency*—surrendering to the inner urge most everyone has to "take it easy"; being satisfied with "good enough" instead of "good," and with "good" instead of "excellent."

*Loss of purpose*—failing to make mental provision or concrete plan for going anywhere else; reaching the first goal becomes the end of the career instead of another beginning.[2]

If you are saying, "You're talking about me,"

please read on, because simply recognizing the problem is a problem half solved. And those who are willing to take some risks, are willing to start believing in themselves once again, will soon discover that life really does begin when they finally get moving.

I will go anywhere provided it is forward.

David Livingstone

# 4

# Life Begins When You Get Moving

Are you prepared mentally, physically, and spiritually to challenge yourself to success? I hope so. If you are, this chapter is meant for you. Starting now there are two options: you can choose to be a winner, or you can decide to be a loser. Two choices. No middle ground. It's like being pregnant: you are or you are not.

Let's take a look at some comparisons between how winners and losers respond to life. Then make your decision.

The winner is always part of the answer; the loser is usually part of the problem.

The winner says, "Come on, let me do it for you"; the loser says, "That's not my job."

The winner sees a green near every sand trap; the loser sees two or three sand traps near every green.

The winner says, "It may be difficult but it's possible"; the loser says, "It may be possible but it's too difficult."

What are you? A winner or a loser?

We can't "win 'em all." But we can consciously choose to be positive, self-motivated individuals who expect the best from ourselves and others. The difference is attitude.

Remember . . . it may be difficult, but it's possible.

*Make time work for you.* If you're a winner, you'll make time work for you. You will harness it and it will become your slave.

Dag Hammarskjold, in his book *Markings,* said, "Life yields only to the conqueror. Never accept what can be gained by giving in. You will be living off stolen goods and your muscles will atrophy. . . . Life only demands from you the strength you possess. Only one feat is possible—not to run away. . . . Time goes by, but reputation increases as ability declines."

A great way to determine how effectively—or ineffectively—we use our time is to take any time-consuming task and try to do it in two-thirds the time. The results may be surprising. Or keep track of how we spend our time for an entire month. The time-wasters will jump off the page.

The list of time-wasters is seemingly endless. Each of us knows what ours are and we should check periodically to determine which of them can be eliminated, adjusted, or minimized: TV-viewing time, idle chatter, unnecessary newspaper or magazine reading, paper shuffling, excessive telephone conversation, longer-than-necessary "in the sack," extra shopping trips, unorganized daily agendas, ad infinitum, ad nauseam. Make a list of time-wasters—and then act on it, one item at a time. The time saved for doing more productive and enjoyable things will be a surprise and a delight. Saving time is a constant challenge for all of us. As Keith Huttenlocker has said, "Be content with what you have, but not with what you are."

*Look for the tough jobs.* Don't be satisfied with a life of mediocrity. Stretch yourself. Pick up where others have failed. We used to think we used only five or six percent of our mental capacity. We now think it may be only one-tenth of one percent. *On a good day!* That's not very impressive when we consider our potential. So go to it!

Breaking the four-minute mile was more a result of mental training than physical. And each of us can break our *own* "four-minute mile" in our individual field of endeavor, because winners *choose* to believe they will break the record long before their bodies *allow* them to do it. Why? Because they believe in themselves. It's all part of motivation to last a lifetime.

Denis Waitley, in his powerful book *The Winner's Edge,* gives a convincing list of ten self-esteem action reminders. A winner bent on breaking some personal records will accept them—and act on them—without batting an eye. Waitley suggests:

1. *Dress and look your best at all times* regardless of the pressure from your friends and peers. . . .

2. *Take inventory of your good reasons for self-esteem* today. Write down your blessings, who and what you are thankful for; accomplishments, what you have done that you are proud of so far. . . .

3. *Set your own internal standards* rather than comparing yourself to others. Accept yourself as you are right now, but keep upgrading your own standards, lifestyle, behavior, professional accomplishments.

4. *Volunteer your own name first* in every telephone call and whenever you meet someone new. By paying value to your own name in communication, you are developing the habit of paying value to yourself as an individual.

5. *Respond with a simple, courteous "thank you"* when anyone pays you a compliment for any reason.

6. *Use encouraging affirmative language* when you talk to yourself and to others about yourself. Focus on uplifting and building adjectives and adverbs. Everything you say about yourself is being recorded by others, and more importantly by your own self-image.

7. *Sit down and list your best attributes.* List positive alternatives to habits you seriously want to change. Seek out authorities with proven records of success after whom to model your winning habits.

8. *Look people in their eyes.* When you speak to anyone for any reason, concentrate on direct eye contact. It is one of the most important nonverbal

indicators of self-confidence.

9. *Keep a self-development plan ongoing* at all times. Sketch it out on paper.

10. *Smile!* In every language, in every culture, it is the light in your window that tells people that there's a caring, sharing individual inside, and it's the universal code for "I'm okay, and you're super, too!"[1]

Make every day a challenge to be better than you were the day before. Trust a great God to help you develop every bit of potential He has given you. Believe with all your heart you can be a person with motivation to last a lifetime.

W. Clement Stone said that any person can become a success. He insisted that success is something that lies within, and to achieve it we must begin by changing ourselves. He told this story to make his point:

One rainy day a preacher was trying to prepare his sermon and, at the same time, take care of his young son while his wife was out shopping.

The boy was restless and bored and kept interrupting his dad.

Finally the minister picked up a magazine and found a map of the world inside. He ripped out the page, tore it into small pieces, and scattered them on the floor.

"Johnny," he said, "if you can put this back together right, I'll give you 25 cents."

The boy started in eagerly, and the minister retired to his study, convinced that the youngster would be kept busy the rest of the morning.

But in a few minutes Johnny knocked at the

door, the bits of paper neatly arranged and the map in order.

"Son, how did you do that so fast?" his father gasped.

"It was easy," the boy answered. "On the back of the map was a picture of a man. I laid a sheet of paper on the floor, put together the picture of the man, turned it over, and the map was all together. I figured that if I got the man right, the world would be right."

The minister smiled, handed the boy a quarter, and said, "You've given me my sermon for tomorrow—If a man's right, his world will be right."

The highly motivated man or woman never stops working at "getting the man right." It's all part of developing a motivation to last a lifetime.

We quoted Denis Waitley earlier on self-esteem. Here are Waitley's ten action reminders for the "motivated winner."

1. *Wake up happy.* Optimism and pessimism are behavioral attitudes. Listen to a motivational tape on your way to work. Read educational and inspirational books and articles that give you a lift the first thing in the morning. [And, we would add, begin your day with prayer and reading God's Word.]

2. *Use positive self-talk from morning to bedtime.* "It's another good day for me." "Things usually work out my way." "I expect a great year." "Next time I'll do better." "We'll make it."

3. *Look at problems as opportunities.* Make a list of your most pressing problems, the ones that block your professional and personal fulfillment. Write a one or two sentence definition of each problem.

Now rewrite the definition, only this time view it as an opportunity or exercise to challenge your creativity and ingenuity.

4. *Concentrate all your energy and intensity without distraction on the successful completion of your current, most important project.* Forget about the consequences of failure. Failure is only a temporary change in direction to set you straight for your next success. Remember, you usually get what you think of most. Finish what you start.

5. *Find something good in all of your personal relationships* and accentuate the blessings or lessons in even the most trying confrontations.

6. *Learn to stay relaxed and friendly* no matter how much tension you are under.

7. *Think and speak well of your health.* Teach yourself and your children to use positive self-talk about your health.

8. *Expect the best from others, too!* Two of the keys to leadership are encouragement and praise. It's contagious!

9. *This week seek and talk in person to someone who is currently doing what you want to do most and doing it well.*

10. *The best way to remain optimistic is to associate with winners and optimists. You can be realistic and optimistic at the same time by realistically examining the facts of a situation, while remaining optimistic about your ability to contribute to a solution or a constructive alternative.*[2]

These are the goals of a person in love with life—motivated to be every inch the person God created him or her to be.

Remember that all of us are always motivated in some direction, and this motivation is directed toward some goal or objective. We need to check frequently to make certain that ours will honor Christ and be beneficial not only—or primarily—to ourselves but to those with whom we live and work as well.

You cannot kindle a fire in any heart until it is burning in your own.

# 5

# Leaders and Motivation

---

**M**axwell Maltz, author of the four-million-copy best seller *Psycho-Cybernetics*, has perhaps done more in recent years to remind us of the importance of maintaining a healthy self-image than almost any other writer. To people of all ages, Dr. Maltz says, "You are embarking on the greatest adventure of your life—to improve your self-image, to create more meaning in your life and in the lives of others. This is your responsibility. Accept it, now!"

Though what he says is important for every human being, it is of paramount importance for the man or woman who must lead others. As a corollary to this, in his *Thoughts to Live By*, Dr.

Maltz lists what he calls his daily dozen—twelve attitudes that are essential to maintain a strong sense of personal motivation.

1. Love. Without it, we cannot survive. This incorporates love between man and woman and the psychological and spiritual love of mankind, which is the foundation upon which we build Brotherhood.

2. Security. There is a need for financial security, but there is also a very great need for emotional and spiritual security within oneself that will provide peace of mind.

3. Self-expression. We need to do something creative in this world instead of being just idle bystanders. (Let me suggest that many leaders are leaders in name only. If you're a leader, don't just stand there . . . *Lead!*)

4. Recognition. We must feel acceptance by others, but first we must find acceptance within ourselves and recognize our own worth.

5. New creative experiences. These determine our growth and maturity. We must continually remain alert for new opportunities to express ourselves creatively.

6. Self-respect. More than anything else, we should value self-respect and the respect of others and for others.

7. Getting more living out of life. Instead of being passive vegetables, we must create a richer life, each on his own terms, by his own standards.

8. Sharing happiness with others. Man should value his capacity to give.

9. Involvement. Here is one of the essential requirements for people of all ages. Seek to help

others who need your courage, your understanding, your good will.

10.  The art of relaxation. We need to get rid of our tensions and recharge our creative energies for peace.

11.  Reaching goals. It is through reaching daily goals that we reach personal success and maturity.

12.  Rising above a mistake. We must learn to see the errors in daily life and we must learn to forgive ourselves so that we can approach new goals with clarity of mind and conscience.[1]

But let's qualify our definition of leader before we go any further. We certainly go beyond the dictionary explanation, which says a leader is a "guiding or directing head, as of an army or political group." If the definition were to remain that narrow, this chapter would have little significance for the average reader.

So before anyone says, "This chapter's not for me," consider how each of us is a leader.

Mothers and fathers are setting daily examples to their children from morning to night. The cliché is still true: What we do speaks so loudly our children often cannot hear what we say.

This truism applied positively is a basic lesson in education. Most of what we learn happens at an informal, unconscious level. It follows that the way we "teach" people is by letting them observe what needs to be done and how to do it as we go about our basic, everyday business of doing our job. A requirement of leadership is to train (educate), and a basic method of training is modeling. This is most particularly true for those of us who have the responsibility of parenting. Quite likely few of us understand the tremendous effect modeling as mothers and fathers has on our offspring.

Those who coach high school football, basketball, or tennis teams are well aware that students see coaches as role models. What kind of a leader do they see? One who teaches "win at any cost" or one who counsels "play—and at the same time 'learn the game of life'?"

The late Paul "Bear" Bryant, football's winningest coach, was more than a coach. He was a father figure, model, exhorter, disciplinarian. It was terribly important to him that his footballers first and foremost receive a quality education at his school, the University of Alabama. He desired to build men as much, or more, than to win football games. This is what his players would look back on with deep appreciation ten or twenty years after their football careers were over.

As a pastor, Sunday school teacher, or youth leader, how we lead others is shaping their lives forever. Obviously, we will not be perfect. We will sometimes grow in ten directions at once and thus perhaps feel we are sounding an "uncertain trumpet." Yet, in spite of the pressures and tensions in our lives, we must continue to lead effectively and creatively.

How do you—how do we—do this? With a life filled with uncertainties, problems, obstacles, and frustrations, how do we maintain the spirit and drive essential to leadership? By first kindling that unquenchable fire in our own souls—the kind of fire that not only warms us, but that also is felt by all with whom we come in contact—families, students, colleagues, or employees.

Let's look at you the business person for a moment. You know that motivating others to do good, productive work (a subject of our next chapter) is seldom easy and that it's not purely mechanical. Further, there is no guaranteed formula for success in motivating employees. You also know it's hard just to keep yourself motivated.

But there are ways to maintain a healthy philosophy of managing as a *motivator of people* and to communicate that position effectively. One of those ways is to use the following "executive checklist," which was published in the *Hillsdale College Leadership Letter.* Read it carefully and ask yourself, "What do I believe about the people I am attempting to lead?"

Do I see that
- an objective evaluation of myself—both strengths and shortcomings—affects my relationships with the employee?
- I must understand not only my own perceptions but also those of the employee?
- the employee wants to perform his or her job successfully and that I am in a strong position to help?
- the personal and social needs of the employee may be more important than his economic needs?
- I must help the employee to see that company goals are worth striving for?

- I present company goals best when employees see in their achievements the fulfillment of their own goals?
- the teaching of good work habits helps the employee achieve a better image of himself and an improved work record?
- my type of leadership—ranging from restrictive to permissive—contributes to the kind of response I elicit from my employees?
- showing appreciation for work well done is one of the most sought after benefits by the employee?
- all people, including myself, make mistakes . . . and that it is not a sign of weakness to admit it?[2]

Can we say with Andrew Carnegie, "Leave my factories but take away my people and soon grass will grow on my factory floors. Take my factories, but leave me my people and soon we will have new and better plants"?

If we can, we are already far down the line in maintaining a motivation for leadership destined to last a lifetime.

As leaders we know the importance of being creative and innovative. Further, we know how vital it is to continually pursue, develop, and nurture the traits of a leader—those qualities that enable us to exercise extra-special gifts. Among the most important traits are intelligence, dependability, sociability, loyalty, friendliness, and faithfulness.

The following traits are important for all leaders, but they are essential for Christian leaders:

**Enthusiasm.** This trait includes both optimism

and hope. No pessimist ever made a great leader. The pessimist sees a difficulty in every opportunity; the optimist sees great opportunities in every difficulty. An optimist laughs to forget; a pessimist forgets to laugh.

**Trustworthiness.** A Christian leader is honest and transparent with all his or her dealings and relationships. A leader must be worthy of the trust of those who follow; he or she must be a person of integrity—and without compromise.

**Discipline.** Those who are self-disciplined are able to lead others because they have been conquered by Christ's love. Their motivation comes from a relationship with the most disciplined Man who ever walked this earth. Jesus was never too busy to care. His agenda was never so full He couldn't reach out to someone in need. While others slept, Jesus prayed. While others tried to protect Him from "intrusions," Jesus welcomed those "intrusions"—because He had come to heal just those kind of people. Disciplined leaders model the behavior of the Master. While others waste time, they will study. While others play, they will pray.

**Confidence.** If a leader does not or cannot believe in himself or herself, certainly no one else will.

**Decisiveness.** When all the facts are in, a swift and clear decision is the mark of a true leader. Such people will resist the temptation to procrastinate in reaching a decision. Neither will they vacillate once the decision has been made. Indecision in a time of emergency destroys any capacity to lead.

**Courage.** Courage is the hallmark of any leader, and courage of the highest order is an essential quality of the spiritual leader. The highest degree of courage is seen in the person who is most fearful but refuses to capitulate to the fear. The biblical command is to "be of good courage." Courage is the ability to "stay in there five minutes longer!"

**Sense of humor.** Humor is another important trait of an effective leader. Clean, wholesome humor will relax tensions and relieve a difficult situation faster than anything else. A good laugh at ourselves is better than a tonic. It often saves a difficult situation. Incidentally, a good test of the appropriateness of our humor is whether we control it or it controls us.

One of the best examples of this test in my experience has been my dear friend and former mentor, Dr. Bob Cook, now president of The King's College in New York State. His refreshingly original humor and his cleverly crafted but never offensive puns have, time after time, brought a wholesome atmosphere to a tense situation. He is not particularly a "joke teller" but his sense of humor has lightened many a conversation, meeting, or sermon.

**Loyalty.** This important leadership trait should probably be at the top of our list. It is expressed in commitment, steadfastness, and faithfulness to those served.

Many people have latent and undeveloped qualities which, through lack of self-awareness and self-knowledge, may remain long undiscovered. There are thousands of potential leaders who do not yet know they are destined to lead.

J. Oswald Sanders has provided some useful standards of self-measurement to help us detect weaknesses that inhibit our leadership potential. Here are his questions to the would-be leader:

- Have you ever broken yourself of a bad habit? To lead others, one must be master of oneself.
- Do you retain control of yourself when things go wrong? The leader who loses self-control in testing circumstances forfeits respect and loses influence. A leader must be calm in crises and resilient in adversity and disappointment.
- Can you handle criticism objectively and remain unmoved under it?
- Do you turn it to good account? The humble man can derive benefit from petty and even malicious criticism.
- Do you use disappointments creatively?
- Do you possess the ability to secure discipline without having to resort to a show of authority? True leadership is an internal quality of the spirit and requires no external show of force.
- Have you qualified for the beatitude of the peacemaker? It is much easier to keep the peace than to make peace where it has been shattered. An important function in leadership is conciliation—the ability to discover common ground between opposing viewpoints and then induce both parties to accept it . . .
- Can you induce people to do happily some legitimate thing which they would not normally wish to do?

• Do you find it easy to make and keep friends? Your circle of loyal friends is an index of the quality and extent of your leadership.[3]

**Attitude.** When all is said and done, when all the books are read and all the seminars attended, the single leadership quality that ultimately wins the day is attitude.

Most of our problems are self-induced. A motivation for excellence in leadership simply cannot be achieved when there is a negative attitude problem. Seldom is the problem a low IQ, less than brilliant aptitude, or too few university degrees. When we fail to perform as leaders, it is almost always because of our attitude.

Here are some concepts you may find helpful in correcting your own attitudes.

1. Our attitude at the beginning of a job will affect the outcome of the job more than anything else.

2. Our attitude toward life determines life's attitude toward us.

3. Our attitude toward others will determine their attitude toward us.

4. Before we can achieve the kind of life we want, we must think, act, walk, talk, and conduct ourselves in ways characteristic of who we ultimately wish to become.

5. The higher we go in any organization of value, the better the attitude we'll find.

6. Holding successful, positive thoughts in our minds will make all the difference in the world.

7. If we always make a person feel needed, im-

portant, and appreciated, he or she will return this attitude to us.

8. Part of a good attitude is to look for the best in new ideas. So look for good ideas everywhere. We will find them in the most wonderful places: on the bumpers of cars, on restaurant menus, in books, in travel—out of the innocent mouths of children.

9. Don't broadcast personal problems. It probably won't help you, and it cannot help others.

10. Don't talk about your health unless it's good.

11. Radiate the attitude of well-being. Don't be embarrassed to share visions, desires, and goals.

12. Treat everyone with whom you come in contact as a fellow member of the human race—with all the rights, duties, and privileges thereof. The Golden Rule still applies: Do unto others as you would have them do unto you.

Everyone in the world is unique. There never has been another you, nor will there ever be one. Even twins don't have identical fingerprints. It follows that each of us has different stress needs in different areas of life. We need to know ourselves well enough so that we can apply our gifts and skills in ways that will strengthen us through stress rather than weaken us through distress. The apostle Paul put this in the right context in Romans 12: "Do not think of yourself more highly than you ought, but rather think of yourself with sober judgment, in accordance of the measure of faith God has given you." This is not to admonish us; rather it is to encourage us to accept who we are. Does it not follow that Christians, of all people, should be able to accept themselves and each other, to see that their gifts and experience are given to them as stewards of God's good grace?

We need to accept ourselves—and others. This is not easy to do, particularly in a western society that continually calls us to become something we are not, whether it is to be more handsome, more beautiful, the owner of a prestige automobile, or a friend of "the beautiful people." The whole point of advertising is to make us dissatisfied with ourselves.

God is not playing games with us. He is the One who is *for* us. We need to accept our position in life, and that of others as well, not in the sense that we cannot move forward, but rather that at this moment we are who we are and that God is able to use us where we are. How wonderful to know that we are all loved by Him—and He *likes* us as well!

My friend Dr. Robert H. Schuller gave the following excellent suggestions in a taped lecture on leadership:

> Principle Number One: Be prepared to pay for the help you need. You say you can't afford it? You probably can't afford *not* to spend the money to hire top quality people.
>
> Principle Number Two: Be a team builder, not an empire builder. Today's great executives build their companies and the people in them more than they build their own names and create their own empires. Today's wise senior executive sees himself as

the quarterback of a winning team, not an empire builder exploiting for his own glory and wealth the talents and abilities of his associates.

Principle Number Three: Offer your people exciting, pace-setting challenges. If you want to get top people on your team, promise them the chance to join in creating something bigger and better than anything done before.

Principle Number Four: Give your teammates freedom. Yes, the greatest people are attracted by the greatest challenges, but they must have the promise of greater freedom to create and find new and better answers. Promise them the freedom to dream, to imagine, to plan. Having the freedom to shoot for the biggest, the best, the most worthwhile, generates maximum energy and inspires unbelievable dedication.

Principle Number Five: Determine in your mind that you will never take a chance on losing a good teammate once you have him or her on the team.

Principle Number Six: Learn to live with difficult people. Learn from them and learn to work with them. Some of the people we may have to depend on in order to solve our problems or achieve our dreams may be difficult to get along with. But learn to appreciate them. Don't be afraid to work with people who at times may be disagreeable.

Principle Number Seven: Learn to deal constructively with disagreements.

It is obvious that not everyone, at all times, is going to agree with us. And that's all right![4]

Do you recall Barnabas and Paul as recorded in the Book of Acts? Here were two very different men. People saw them together and wondered why they stuck together as they did. They had been friends for a number of years. The older had opened many doors for the younger. When others had thought the younger man was a braggart and upstart, the older man had seen his depth and brilliance. Paul, the younger, was argumentative and he usually won. He was disdainful of those who weren't willing to give their all for the work. The older man, Barnabas, was from a different mold. He didn't have a great deal of brilliance, but he did have a great deal of warmth. He, too, was a leader, but a different type. There wasn't much doubt about who was the more outstanding. By education, dedication, and capability Paul outstripped Barnabas. People often wondered why the older man had asked for the younger to help him. Wouldn't he soon be outstripped? Soon the two were peers, and a few years later the older was working for the younger. Eventually their different approach to things brought such sharp differences of opinion that they could no longer work together. The stress was too much.

We suspect that when Barnabas introduced Paul to the apostles he saw in Paul a man with gifts far superior to his own. When he sought him out at Tarsus and brought him to Antioch, he did it because of those various gifts. What would have happened to the course of history had Barnabas not had the insight and willingness to put another person forward?

Recognizing the gifted person who needs a guide is perhaps a gift in itself. There are indeed special people whom God has prepared to stimulate us, prod us, lead us, challenge us, and gently move us out of the status quo. It is this matter of how we motivate other people that we want to discuss in our next chapter.

> Setting an example is not the main means of influencing another, it is the *only* means.
> Albert Einstein

# 6

# How to Motivate People

The party aboard ship was in full swing. Speeches were being made by the captain, the crew, and the guests enjoying the week-long voyage. Sitting at the head table was a seventy-year-old man who, somewhat embarrassed, was doing his best to accept the praise being poured on him.

Earlier that morning a young woman had apparently fallen overboard, and within seconds this elderly gentleman was in the cold, dark waters at her side. The woman was rescued and the elderly man became an instant hero.

When time finally came for the brave passenger to speak, the stateroom fell into a hush as he rose from his chair. He went to the microphone and, in what was probably the shortest "hero's" speech ever offered, spoke these stirring words: "I just want to know one thing—who pushed me?"

Sound familiar? As a leader have you resorted to this kind of motivational technique? Have you, out of sheer frustration, pushed your employees, members of your parish, or your own children "overboard" to get done what *you* wanted done?

Guilt for such an approach certainly has fallen on all our heads at one time or another—but we know it is hardly the way to build *esprit de corps* among people with whom we work. There are many ways to get people to work harder, produce more, and become a part of a successful business, church, school, or home. But pushing them overboard is not one of them!

Dr. Mortimer R. Feinberg, an industrial psychologist, believes that almost every manager's success as a leader and motivator is directly related to how sincerely he demonstrates his concern for his people. He writes, "The best way to motivate a subordinate is to show him that you are conscious of his needs, his ambitions, his fears and himself as an individual. The insensitive manager who is perhaps unintentionally aloof, cold, impersonal and uninterested in his staff, usually finds it very difficult to get his people to put out any extra effort."

In his book *Effective Psychology for Managers*, Feinberg offers us some fine suggestions.

He suggests that perhaps it would be helpful to

look at the negative side first to see what "demotivates" businessmen, pastors, teachers, parents—anyone who is a model or example to others. Here is a modified version of Feinberg's guidelines to avoid "de-motivating" subordinates.

1. Never belittle a subordinate. No person likes to think that others regard him or her as stupid or inept or unable to handle the job. In most cases you can talk with an employee, a student, a son or daughter without using such red-flag words as lazy, sloppy, indifferent. Such words are steamroller words. They flatten and destroy initiative and self-esteem.

2. Never criticize a subordinate in front of others. To do so is a cardinal sin of management. You'll be tempted to do it to "set an example to the others who also might need to hear it," but you'll live to regret it. And your employee may not forgive you, especially after he or she has left your organization and tells others how *you* treat people.

3. Never fail to give your people your undivided attention. It may not be your job to give others your every waking moment, but from time to time take people into the privacy of your office to ask how things are going. If this is not possible because of the size of your organization, encourage your department heads to make it a practice. Loyalty to you and to your organization will be fostered when you take the time to be genuinely interested.

4. Never seem preoccupied with your own interests. Your future may very well be your primary

concern, but try not to communicate this to others. Allow those around you to share the credit for work well done.

5. Never play favorites. Here's another cardinal rule of good management. When you start to make exceptions because of your own personal preferences, the rest of your staff will pick up on this faster than you can say, "I didn't mean it, folks!"

6. Never fail to help your people grow. Fight for your employees, your children, those you care about. Be an encouragement to them. Let them see you have their best interests at heart. And if you really do, they will see it. Let them know you're on their side.

7. Never be insensitive to small things. Don't make loose or rash statements. Here's an extreme example: A supervisor in a company had a terrible reputation among his department's employees. To top it off, one day he roared in a fit of temper, "I don't care how long you've been in this firm. Seniority means nothing in my department." This company had been without a union for seventy-five years, but with this crack in management's armor, the union finally gained admittance. Its organizing propaganda theme: "Seniority means nothing."

8. Never embarrass people who might just be learning the ropes. Just because *you* can do the job better, faster, and with more flair, don't do it at the expense of your employee, child, or member of your congregation. It is important to a person's dignity to be able to do something well on his or

her own. When you jump in to do it yourself, you pop the balloon. In short, you are putting into practice the best example of "de-motivation."

9. Never vacillate in making a decision. It is a sign of strength in supervision and management to be able to make decisions promptly and wisely. As a leader you must stick your neck out. If the people around sense you are afraid to do so, they too will lack the confidence to make decisions in their own areas of work. Vacillate in your decision making and your whole motivation effort will crumble around you.[1]

But enough for understanding what "demotivates." Let's turn to the positive—to proven ways to motivate people on a day-to-day basis. Overall, we think you'll find they add up to effective management.

1. Communicate standards and be consistent. When a person knows he is being evaluated according to a single, fair standard, he or she has a target to shoot for.

2. Be aware of your own biases and prejudices. No one is without biases. The question is whether or not you are aware of your prejudices. How can you become more aware? One way is to keep a record of your prejudices. Check to see if your "prejudgments" are accurate. If not, then change your attitude about that person. Invariably, emotional reactions color what should be effective, objective judgments. Be aware of yours.

3. Let people know where they stand. Carry out regular performance reviews. The positive or nega-

tive thoughts you have rattling about in your head serve no useful purpose to your people if you never tell them. Give each person sufficient attention. Let each man or woman, boy or girl, know you are looking for ways in which they can better themselves. Your honesty—spoken in positive, self-esteem-enhancing ways—will create an atmosphere of trust. And without that, you could end up being the only passenger on your ship.

4.  Give praise when it is appropriate. Properly handled, praise is one of the best motivation factors available to you as a leader. Avoid giving praise for every little thing done, because this will make your praise meaningless. Like any good seasoning, a little goes a long way.

5.  Keep people informed of changes that may affect them. If you plan to move your warehouse within a year, don't wait until the moving vans arrive to tell your people. You don't have to divulge every company secret, but it's evidence of your concern if you keep your employees *appropriately* informed.

6.  Care about your employees. If you have a suggestion box in the coffee room—or if you ask for comments from your church members, children, or students—then by all means *read those suggestions* and *listen to the comments.* If you don't, they'll know it's no more than an idle exercise in your attempt to *pretend* you're interested.

7.  See people as ends, not means. The conductor of an orchestra regards his players as individuals, but what kind of a concert would one big

trumpet solo be? When explorer Thomas Cook discovered a new island, he named the discovery after the first man who spotted it. He regarded every man in his crew, even the ship's boy, as a partner in the adventure. If you are to succeed as a leader, Cook's example is a good one to remember.

8. Build independence. This is closely tied to caring for the people with whom you work. And yet, it is often a most frightening approach for managers to take. If their people feel overly independent, they fear they will lose control. Actually, quite the opposite will occur. If you encourage a good worker to become independent, he or she will become more loyal to you and to your organization. But try to keep a good person in a box and see what happens.

One of my favorite quotations in all of American history is the word from one of my heroes, Theodore Roosevelt, who wrote in 1899:

> It is not the critic who counts; not the man who points out how the strong man stumbled or where the doer of deeds could have done them better. The credit belongs to the man who is actually in the arena; whose face is marred by dust and sweat and blood; who strives valiantly; who errs, and comes up short again and again, because there is no effort without error and shortcoming; who does actually try to do the deed; who knows the great enthusiasm, the great devotion and spends himself in a worthy cause; who, at the worst, if he fails, at least fails while daring greatly.
>
> Far better it is to dare mighty things, to win

glorious triumphs even though checkered by failure, than to rank with those poor spirits who neither enjoy nor suffer much because they live in the gray twilight that knows neither victory or defeat.

Or, again, as President Coolidge once wrote:

Press on: nothing in the world can take the place of persistence. Talent will not; nothing is more common than unsuccessful men with talent. Genius will not; unrewarded genius is almost a proverb. Education will not; the world is full of educated derelicts. Persistence and determination alone are overwhelmingly powerful.

9. Exhibit personal diligence. There has never been a successful supervisor or executive—a man or woman who could motivate others—who did not exhibit the qualities of self-motivation and commitment. You just won't find it. You motivate by example. Believe it or not, employees—even children, sometimes—actually like to feel as though they are living up to the image of their boss—especially if the boss is devoted to the job of making his or her enterprise a smashing success. The people around you *want* to be a part of the success you are creating. And don't forget it!

10. Be willing to learn from others. Be honest with yourself. You don't know it all—no matter how smart you are. There's always someone, someplace who knows more about something than you do. Not to admit this could limit your potential for production and certainly reduce your impact

on the marketplace or society. The old adage remains true: You can do just about anything you want if you don't care who gets the credit.

11. Demonstrate confidence. Show by your behavior and language that you are confident of your own abilities—and that you share that same confidence with those who work or live with you.

Part of the Christian's motivation is a God-placed longing to help others. As the Scripture puts it, "Good men long to help each other" (Prov. 12:12 LB). There is nothing that builds *esprit de corps* within the family, the church, the business, the ministry, or the community more than expressions of mutual confidence. Once we indicate that we believe in the other person's integrity, motivation, and personhood, we form a bond as strong as individual pieces of wire strung together to make a cable.

12. Delegate, delegate, delegate. The leader who creates, delegates, and moves on to still more creative activity, will find himself or herself leading the pack. But woe to the leader who must know every detail, every purchase order, and the daily schedule of every employee. The inability to delegate has been proven again and again to be the most common reason for leadership failure. Are you willing to turn loose some of your responsibility? If you do, you'll find you're really not giving it away at all.

13. Encourage ingenuity. This technique works with everyone. Even the lowest-paid clerk can be creative. Challenge the people who work or live

with you to "beat your system." If, for example, your filing system leaves something to be desired, don't *you* change it. Have others recommend the changes. You will literally change the atmosphere of your office. You'll also be surprised at the wealth of ideas generated. And as you begin to think of and develop it, you will find that such a list is endless. Go to it!

> All things are possible to him
> who believes.
>
> **Jesus Christ**

# 7

# The Greatest Motivator
# of All Time

---

He was born in an obscure village, the child of a peasant woman. He grew up in still another village, where he worked in a carpenter shop until he was thirty. Then for three years *he was an itinerant preacher.*

He never wrote a book.

He never held an office.

He never had a family or owned a house.

He didn't go to college.

He never traveled 200 miles from the place where he was born. He did none of the things one usually associates with greatness.

*He had no credentials but himself.*

He was only 33 when public opinion turned against him. His friends ran away. He was turned over to his enemies and went through the mockery of a trial. *He was nailed to a cross between two thieves.*

When he was dying, his executioners gambled for his clothing, the only property he had on earth. When he was dead, he was laid in a borrowed grave through the pity of a friend.

Nineteen centuries have come and gone, and today he is the central figure of the human race, *the leader of mankind's progress.*

All the armies that ever marched, all the navies that ever sailed, all the parliaments that ever sat, all the kings that ever reigned, put together, have not affected the life of man on earth as much as that One Solitary Life.                    (Anonymous)

What was it about Jesus that He could take a band of poor, unschooled Galilean provincials and use them to light a revolution of love that continues to burn in the hearts of men and women throughout our world?

How was Jesus able to approach Matthew, the tax collector, with a simple "Follow me," to which Matthew responded by leaving his occupation to become a follower of the Master?

What about Zacchaeus' response to Jesus? Jesus saw the little man high up in a sycamore tree trying to get a better look at what was going on. Zacchaeus undoubtedly thought he was safe from the scrutiny of Jesus, when suddenly he was ordered to come down from the tree because Jesus announced, "I'm going to your house today." He got down. And Jesus *did* go to his house.

What was there about the character of Jesus

that He could, with a sentence of rebuke, turn away a mob intent on stoning a woman caught in the act of adultery?

Throughout the gospel record there is a listing of an incredible variety of places to which Jesus went and people to whom He ministered.

Of course He preached to the crowds in the synagogues. We would expect that. But He also was found at the seaside with the fishermen. He moved among unclean lepers. He scourged the temple of the moneychangers. (Here was certainly no "gentle Jesus, meek and mild.") He went into the wheat fields with the harvesters and told them of the bread of life that He represented.

In the crowd, He sensed when the woman with the issue of blood touched His garment. He sat beside the man with the withered hand and made Him complete and whole. He broke bread at the Pharisee's table where a woman of the street came in to wash His feet with her tears. He sat with the Samaritan woman at Sychar's well and told her of the water of life that could quench her thirst eternally. She came to the well with her waterpot—and went away with the well itself!

In all of His life and ministry, Jesus motivated people to action in response to His acts of grace and goodness. He loved them—and He loves you and me!

Not only did Jesus have an overwhelming love for people, He also loved life itself. He was interesting and interested. Jesus observed everything around him. He saw the trees and flowers more intently than anyone else ever could have seen them. The Gospels are filled with the great outdoors.

In his inspirational book *That Man Is You,* Louis Evely says this of Jesus:

> He looked through everything and discovered the divine reality on which it'd been patterned. He really saw the world and loved it.
>
> For example, at the sight of water, whether in a lake or in a fountain, He'd muse: "Water's a good thing."
>
> "Give me some water," He asked the Samaritan woman but added, "If you only knew the water I can give you—real water, living water, water that'll quench your thirst forever."
>
> To the least promising of men He showed such love, such unwonted and compelling trust, that they'd become dazzling founts of generosity and faith.[1]

This was Jesus of Nazareth. The Son of Man. The example of God-incarnate to be the model for all civilizations to come.

With all due respect to poet Swinburne, Jesus was hardly the "pale Galilean." And the world has not "grown grey" from his breath. Motivators of men and women are not pale copies of a good idea, and the scenery doesn't become grey because they've been there.

Jesus brought color, energy, and life to His surroundings. He could see a small child who hadn't been loved nearly enough, so He loved that boy or girl. When the temple was being misused as a marketplace, it was no mild-mannered, "pale Galilean" who angrily set God's house in order. When accused of wining and dining with sinners, prostitutes, and ne'er-do-wells, Jesus pleaded guilty. He reminded His accusers He had come to bring healing to those who were sick.

Evely also wrote:

> God loves those to whom He can give most, those who expect most from Him, who are most open to Him, need Him most and rely on Him most for everything. Little He cares whether they're as pure as Saint John or as sinful as Mary Magdalene or Zacchaeus.
>
> All that matters to Him is that they like to depend on Him, to rejoice in Him and live through Him alone.[2]

Jesus, Son of God, the author of creativity, motivated men and women to action by his sheer presence. He simply could not be ignored. Of all men in history, Jesus truly was a Man for all seasons.

*Jesus was positive.* The first question Jesus asked the man by the pool was, "Do you want your health restored?" (John 5:6, Moffatt). An important question to us all. Do we want to be well? Do we want to live up to our potential? To do good things—the right things? If so, then every one of God's marvelous resources is at our disposal. Just for the asking.

*Jesus was creative.* He motivated people to action by using illustrations and parables to preach great truths: the unforgiving servant; the sower and the seed; the mustard seed and the yeast; the hidden treasure and the pearl; the landowner and the tenants; the ten virgins; the talents; the wise and foolish builders, and on and on. Unforgettable teaching!

*Jesus knew the source of happiness.* Happiness comes not through what happens to people, but through what people do for others.

Jesus' beautiful teachings of the Beatitudes in Matthew 5 are lessons to be learned and relearned.

> Blessed are the poor in spirit,
>   for theirs is the kingdom of heaven.
> Blessed are those who mourn,
>   for they will be comforted.
> Blessed are the meek,
>   for they will inherit the earth.
> Blessed are those who hunger and thirst for
>     righteousness,
>   for they will be filled.
> Blessed are the merciful,
>   for they will be shown mercy.
> Blessed are the pure in heart,
>   for they will see God.
> Blessed are the peacemakers,
>   for they will be called sons of God.
> Blessed are those who are persecuted because
>     of righteousness,
>   for theirs is the kingdom of heaven.

*Jesus prayed for strength and guidance.* We are reminded to believe, "I can do all things through Christ who strengthens me."

*Jesus lived by his priorities.* He didn't have

much time on earth, so He made the time He had count. He was committed to telling the people of His day about the Kingdom, and His commitment was one hundred percent. The world notices that kind of commitment. Jesus had but one purpose—to declare the good news that sins *could* be forgiven . . . and that man *could* be made whole. It was the best news people had ever heard, and it was irresistible. Truth motivates. Truth wrapped in enthusiasm motivates even more.

Why did people flock to Jesus? For all kinds of reasons. But perhaps the most important reason of all was because Jesus chose to be their friend. And what He said, did, and lived is example enough for us today. Just ask any ten people what they want most in life, and you'll find the majority saying, "I want a real friend."

In a recent issue of the inspiring monthly notes published by the Christophers, I noted these helpful comments on "Ways to Nourish Friendship."

- Permit your friends to be themselves. Accept them as they are. Be grateful for what is there, not annoyed by what friends can't give. Accept each one's imperfections—and individuality—and don't feel threatened if their opinions and tastes sometimes differ from yours.
- Give each other space. We are entitled to our private feelings and thoughts. Friends who try to invade the inner space of one another risk destroying the relationship.
- Be ready to give and to receive. Be eager to help

and be able to ask for help as well. But don't be overdemanding or let yourself be used.

- Make your advice constructive. When a friend needs to talk, listen without interruption. If advice is asked for, be positive and supportive.
- Be loyal. Loyalty is faithfulness. It means "being with" your friend in bad times as well as in good. It means honoring confidence. It means neither disparaging a friend in his absence nor allowing others to do so.
- Give praise and encouragement. Tell your friends what you like about them, how thankful you are for their presence in your life. Delight in their talents, applaud their successes.
- Be honest. Open communication is of the essence of friendship. Express your feelings, good and bad, instead of bottling up your anger or anxiety. Clearing the air helps a relationship grow. But be aware of what is better left unsaid.
- Treat friends as equals. In true friendship there is no Number One, no room for showing off how smart and successful you are, for envy, for feeling superior or inferior.
- Trust your friends. We live in a messy, imperfect world made up of imperfect people. Trust can be betrayed but trust is essential to friendship. Make the effort to believe in the intrinsic goodness of your friends.
- Be willing to risk. One of the obstacles to a close relationship is the fear of rejection and hurt. We don't want to reveal our vulnerability. But unless we dare to love others, we condemn ourselves to a sterile life.[3]

Jesus—the greatest motivator of men and

women who ever lived—knew how to be a friend. And friendship is one of the greatest things we can strive for. It must be part of our strategy to achieve motivation to last a lifetime.

> You will never stub your toe standing still. The faster you go, the more chance there is of stubbing your toe, but the more chance you have of getting somewhere.
>
> Charles F. Kettering

# 8

# A Heart-to-Heart Talk on Motivation

Previous chapters have indicated both the vital importance of being motivated for profitable living—profitable unto God and for ourselves—and of seeking the keys to motivate others. But the question may still remain, What is motivation?

Management expert Peter Drucker says in one of his books, "We really know nothing about motivation," and then goes on for pages to explain what he understands motivation to be! Motivation is a good bit like Mark Twain's weather, "There's a lot of talk about it, but little or no action regarding it."

We have all known people who are motivated to do certain things, and, likewise, those who are *not* motivated to do certain things.

How many times have you heard someone say, "If only I could motivate my kids" or "Nothing seems to motivate him—or her" or "Those people just don't seem to be motivated at all" or "How can I motivate my staff?"?

We tend to think of motivation as an either/or entity. We are either motivated to serve on a committee or we are not. We see some individuals as motivated, and others as not. This view can cause problems because we evaluate an individual's motivation on the basis of the *situation* we are observing.

We need to recognize that every individual is motivated by certain things and, likewise, everyone is motivated to do something. Often the people we see as unmotivated actually are simply not interested in doing the things we are motivated to do. Thus, it is *our* interests that become the guideline for assessing another's motivation when, in fact, that person may be highly motivated to perform some other task. It takes a good leader to find out what it is that motivates others. There is no such thing as an unmotivated person. We are either motivated to do something or motivated *not* to do that thing.

As we deal with other people we ought not spend time fretting about *how* to motivate them, but rather find out what already *does* motivate them. It is not our task to strive constantly to motivate individuals to do what we want them to do, but rather to discover the motivations that already reside within them. I suggest that we find out what motivates us and then go out and discover what motivates others.

What is it that motivates Ted Engstrom? Generally, it is my goals. What "de-motivates" me? Often it is the goals of others. The best motivation is not imposed upon a group or an individual, but discovered and developed from within that group.

How we use motivational factors depends on what really motivates us. Those who are motivated by the flesh view people as resources to make their programs work and themselves look good. If motivated by the Holy Spirit, we view people as a responsibility to be served—to liberate them from bondage to their unmet needs so they can become healthy, growing children of God who are increasingly glorifying Him.

In all matters of motivation, we must ask ourselves if our intention is to bring glory to God. Properly motivating others in this direction is to motivate them into a path of blessing. The greatest motivation in all the world is for a human being to go into business with the Lord God Himself. Then, like the apostle Paul, we can say, "I press on toward the goal to win the prize for which God has called me heavenward in Christ Jesus" (Phil. 3:14).

People are motivated by achievement, by recognition of their efforts, by challenging work, by being made responsible, and by experiencing personal growth. People are "de-motivated" by poor administration, weak supervision, bad working conditions, poor interpersonal relationships, and the absence of status and security. The question of how to motivate others is something people never stop asking. The reason for this is quite simple: Motivation is human energy—the most plentiful and powerful resource on earth. It is the fuel that runs all social organizations from nations to families to individuals. We can never run out of it, yet we never seem to have enough.

The key to motivation is to bring together within the body or organization people who share the same goals. If the organization's goals are freely accepted by members, we have made a major step toward motivated action. And, if the primary goal is to glorify God, lack of motivation will be a problem only when the goal becomes obscured.

Genuine motivation cannot be bought and sold. We can offer someone a million dollars to do something, but that's not motivation; it's bribery. We can hold a gun to someone's head and he or she will most likely do whatever we ask. But that's not motivation; it's intimidation.

A major part of the Christian's motivation is a God-placed longing to help others. As the Scripture puts it, "Good men long to help each other" (Prov. 12:12 LB).

May the ultimate motivational force in all of our lives be to bring glory and honor to "him who loves us and has freed us from our sins by his blood, and has made us to be a kingdom and priests to serve his God and Father—to him be glory and power for ever and ever! Amen" (Rev. 1:5–6).

# Notes

## Chapter 1

[1]Victor E. Frankl, *Man's Search for Meaning* (New York: Pocket Books, 1980), 104–105.

## Chapter 2

[1]"Advice to a (Bored) Young Man," *Newsweek* (February 13, 1967).

## Chapter 3

[1]From *Supervisory Control*, newsletter of The Research Institute of America, Inc., (New York, October 1968).
[2]*Sales Management*, (December 15, 1961), 45–46.

## Chapter 4

[1]Denis Waitley, *The Winner's Edge: How to Develop the Critical Attitude of Success* (New York: Berkley, 1983).
[2]Ibid.

*Chapter 5*

[1]Maxwell Maltz, *Thoughts to Live By* (New York: Pocket Books, 1975), 56–57.

[2]Revised from the *Hillsdale College Leadership Letter*, (Vol. 5, No. 9, February 1967).

[3]J. Oswald Sanders, *Spiritual Leadership* (Chicago: Moody Press, 1967), 26–28.

[4]Robert H. Schuller, "Leadership" (Chicago: Nightingale-Conant Corporation, 1981). Tape recording.

*Chapter 6*

[1]M. R. Feinberg, *Effective Psychology for Managers* (Englewood Cliffs: Prentice-Hall, Inc., 1965).

*Chapter 7*

[1]Louis Evely, *That Man Is You* (Paramus, N.J.: Newman Press, 1964), 95ff.

[2]Ibid., 126ff.

[3]From *Christopher News Notes*, No. 240.